Dorset in the World Wars

by Robert Hesketh

Inspiring Places Publishing
2 Down Lodge Close
Alderholt
Fordingbridge
Hants
SP6 3JA

ISBN 978-0-9955964-6-7
© Robert Hesketh 2019
www.roberthesketh.co.uk

JURASSICCOAST
**QUALITY
BUSINESS**

Contents

Front cover: Top left: Cordite factory workers. Top right: Sherborne ARP wardens.
Bottom: Military funeral, Wareham 1915.
Rear cover: World War II guns at the Nothe Fort, Weymouth.

The First World War

Assembling the Fleet

"No one privileged to witness the sight in ̓
July 1914 will ever forget the mighty armada, reported the southern times,
describing Britain's assembled battle fleets. The message to Germany was
unmistakable: the Royal Navy remained the world's largest war fleet, Britain's
guarantor of security and projection of imperial power.

The causes of the First World War have been hotly disputed ever
since 1914, but a major factor was the naval arms race between the German
and British empires. German naval expansion began in 1898 and was viewed
with increasing alarm by Britain, which responded with her own naval
building programme to maintain the "double power standard", where the
British navy was twice the size of any other.

Meanwhile, events were rapidly building to a crisis in Europe.
Realising the densely packed warships in Weymouth Bay offered a tempting
potential target; Winston Churchill, then First Lord of the Admiralty, ordered
the Second Fleet to its various stations and the Grand Fleet to the safety of
Scapa Flow.

On August 4th Britain declared war. According to the Western
Gazette, Lord Portman, Chairman of Dorset Council, was roundly cheered
for his rousing pro-Government speech: "They (the Government) were bound
to go to war – (hear, hear) – for they could not have deserted France in her
trouble. (Hear, hear.) If they had deserted France at this crisis they could
never have held their heads up again – (applause) – either in Europe or in the
Empire (renewed applause.)"

*HMS Hood before being scuttled on November 4th, 1914 at the
south entrance to Portland Harbour to prevent U-boat attacks.*

Your Country Needs You

Kitchener, the new Secretary of State for War, knew the strength of Germany's massive, well equipped army and foresaw a long war lasting at least three years. Unlike the other major combatants in 1914, Britain did not have compulsory military service and thus a large, trained reserve to draw on. The nation's small professional army would need huge reinforcements and Kitchener appealed for volunteers.

"Weymouth worked itself up into a fever heat of enthusiasm… to back Major Groves and the other recruiting officers in finding a worthy contribution from Weymouth to swell Lord Kitchener's Army," reported the Southern Times on September 5th. Patriotism was a powerful motive for many men joining the long queues at recruiting stations. So too was a thirst for adventure and a desire to escape poorly paid drudgery, which was working life for many. Moreover, the armed forces offered regular pay, regular meals and general applause. Fear of ridicule was spurred by the White Feather Campaign, started in August 1914.

Kitchener's Army, Shaftesbury.

Mobilising for War

Army mobilisation was immediate. Dorchester, home of the Dorsetshire County Regiment, was soon teeming with reservists, Territorials and Yeomanry. Recalled from troubled Ulster, the 1st Battalion of the Dorsets was sent on post haste to France and fought at Mons and on the Marne. They went on to fight in some of the bloodiest battles on the Western Front: First Ypres in 1915; the Somme, 1916; Passchendaele, 1917 and the Last Hundred Days campaign in autumn 1918.

Dorset's five other battalions saw action in several theatres of war. The 2nd Dorsets were sent to Mesopotamia (modern Iraq), where they endured the siege of Kut in 1916 and its terrible aftermath. Of the 350 Dorset

prisoners taken by the Turks, only 70 survived. The 3rd and 4th Dorsets also fought in Mesopotamia and later, Palestine, whilst the 3/4th Battalion served in Ulster and continued there after the Armistice. Gallipoli, the Somme and Passchendaele were among battles fought by the 5th Dorsets. The 6th Battalion was heavily engaged on the Western Front, whilst the Queen's Own Dorset Yeomanry fought in Gallipoli, Egypt and Palestine.

As the Navy had surplus volunteers whilst the Army was desperately short of men, Churchill had the bright idea of forming the Naval Reserve Division to fight on land. Their permanent base was established at Blandford and they trained across Dorset.

We'd never have kom if we'd known der DORSETS were here !

Cartoon postcard acquired in France in World War I.

Wareham in the First World War

Before the start of World War I Wareham was a sleepy town of around 2000 people. The surrounding heathland and its rail connection had, for some years, rendered it a suitable place for training units of the Territorial Army and this led to its being chosen, in September 1914, as the site of a major training camp for Kitchener's new army. A huge camp of wooden huts was constructed either side of Worgret Road on the western side of the town. Regiments from all over Britain trained there as did 'Anzacs' from Australia and New Zealand. After the war the camp was used as a 'tank park' for tanks returning from France; tanks had been developed at nearby Bovington and Lulworth in 1916. The camp closed in 1922; very few traces now remain.

Page 6 top: A view of Wareham Camp, begun in September 1914.
Bottom: A group of engineers practise bridge building.
Page 7 top: A military funeral procession in Wareham, 1915.
Bottom: A group of soldiers in Wareham Camp.

Dorset and Britain's Secret Weapon

Dorset was also chosen for training with Britain's secret new weapon to break the bloody stalemate of trench warfare: "The wooded country around Bovington is particularly adapted to the training of tank battalions," remarked Lt. Colonel Swinton, "the woods and the small streets being very similar to and as equally deserted as the battlefields of France."

Brigadier-General Frederick Gore Anley took charge of the new Tank Training Centre at Bovington Camp in October 1916. There were five tank battalions, each with 72 tanks. Initially, tanks were mainly of shock value, but were used effectively on 19th August 1917 to attack pillboxes at St Julien without a preliminary bombardment. Tanks played a strong role at the Battle of Cambrai in November/December 1917, but came into their own at Amiens (8th August 1918), the battle which launched the Last Hundred Days campaign. British Commander-in-Chief, Sir Douglas Haig commented: "Since the opening of our offensive on 8th August, tanks have been employed in every battle and the importance of the part played by them in breaking the resistance of German infantry can scarcely be exaggerated."

1916 and a 'secret weapon' has overturned on Wool bridge!

Volunteers

Many men engaged in vital war work or too old to enlist in the regular armed forces joined Volunteer Training Battalions, which were added to the county infantry regiment system in 1916. In 1917, members were issued with rifles and machine guns and by 1918 the Volunteer Battalions were 285,000 strong nationally.

Dorset's Volunteer Regiment was formed in 1917 from existing volunteer battalions, with detachments in fourteen towns across the county.

They had several duties, from digging defences to guarding valuable sites, handling munitions, helping with the harvest, firefighting and transporting wounded soldiers.

War Horses

All armies relied heavily on horses, especially for transport. Large numbers were summarily requisitioned. The Dorset County Chronicle reported "Another sharp reminder of the exigencies of war…at many farms horses were seized unceremoniously by the requisition of the military authorities, without regard to the needs of harvesting, and some were even removed from carriers' carts in the streets of Dorchester….and the pick of the stables of many gentlemen in the neighbourhood had to be yielded to the military necessity."

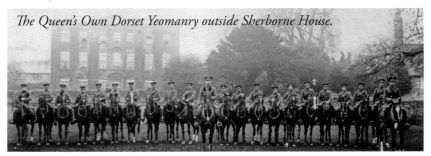

The Queen's Own Dorset Yeomanry outside Sherborne House.

Conscription and Social Control

Military necessity also dictated conscription, as even the host of volunteers - eventually totalling 2.67 million - were inadequate to meet the Army's insatiable demands. Despite strong opposition inside and outside Parliament that compulsory military service was an assault on liberty, conscription was introduced for single men aged 18 to 41 in January 1916 and for married men from May 1916. Dorset men who applied for exemption on various grounds, including health, doing vital war work and conscientious objection had to present their cases before the county's Military Service Tribunal. The local press reported cases.

Fighting a total war also demanded tighter social control. On August 8th, 1914, only four days after declaring war, the British Parliament passed the Defence of the Realm Act (DORA) without debate. Designed to subject civilians to military courts, control communications and Britain's ports, DORA was amended six times during the war and had far reaching consequences for civil liberties. For instance, it instituted a strict blackout, even in counties like Dorset beyond the reach of German airships. British Summer Time was introduced in an effort to drive up productivity by

The Queen's Own Dorset Yeomanry, Cheap Street, Sherborne.

lengthening the working day. Limiting pub opening hours and beer strength had the same object. The act also allowed the Government to seize factories and land to produce the huge quantities of weapons and ammunition essential to win the industrial war of attrition.

DORA also widened police powers and censored speech and writing through this catchall clause: "No person shall by word of mouth or in writing spread reports likely to cause disaffection among any of His Majesty's Forces or among the civilian population."

Anti-war protesters were imprisoned. Letters from the Front were censored and newspaper reports subjected to the Government's Press Bureau. Known to journalists as the Supress Bureau, it controlled reports on troop movements and operational information that could be used by the enemy.

Spy Mania

Breaching DORA could bring custodial, even capital sentences: ten people were executed under its stringent regulations. The threat of espionage induced a climate of fear, but "Spy Mania" had its comic aspects. Major Jarvis of the 3rd Dorsets recalled a shepherd carrying a lantern to lamb his ewes near Wyke was shot at by an over-zealous Army patrol for breaching the blackout.

Jarvis had many such "wild goose chases", but failed to identify a real spy in September 1914. A man claiming to be an American citizen was seen peering into the wire enclosure of Wyke camp. This was part of Portland's extensive defences, designed to protect the world's largest artificial harbour and its facilities, including Whitehead's torpedo works. Naturally, he was arrested. Major Jarvis inspected the man's papers, questioned him, found all in order and released him after a convivial whiskey and soda. His embarrassment may be imagined when the "American" was re-arrested, revealed as German naval officer Carl Lody and thereafter executed.

MI5 records show sixty-five German agents were arrested and convicted during the war. German born shipping clerk Heinrich Schutte, who had lived in England for over 20 years and worked at the Great Western Railway's cargo stage in Weymouth, was arrested and charged with "communicating to another person a sketch, plans, notes …calculated to be useful to the enemy." Schutte's case was withdrawn, probably for lack of evidence, but he was immediately re-arrested, imprisoned and later deported under the Aliens Restriction Act – under which German and Austrian born residents were frequently interned.

Claims that several workers building the new cordite factory at Holton Heath near Poole were German spies proved groundless, but the factory was guarded by armed police nonetheless. Cordite was used as a propellant for shells and Churchill ordered the factory in 1914 to ensure adequate supplies for the Navy. (See page 14.)

Women workers from the Cordite factory, Holton Heath.

Women Workers and Volunteers

Holton Heath was chosen for its relative remoteness and its good access to Poole harbour. Many of the workers were women, which was characteristic of the rapidly expanding munitions industry, where thousands of "munitionettes" found well paid (albeit dangerous) work. Sometimes, this was at new factories, sometimes at expanded facilities such as Whitehead's Torpedo Works at Wyke

Mark 8 Torpedo (WW II) at Portland Harbour.

Regis, where larger and faster torpedoes were developed, with round the clock working for hundreds of people. In other cases, peacetime production was switched to munitions. Channons of Dorchester built cars before the war, but turned to producing gun carriages. Its workforce was almost exclusively female.

Many more women entered employment during the war in a wide variety of roles, including factory workers, farm labourers, bus conductors, clerks, teachers and nursing auxiliaries. Many, particularly middle and upper class women, had their first experience of the working world. Often, they took over from men who had left to fight and entered what had been male preserves. Recognition did not necessarily come easily, as Dorothy Baker found when she became Dorchester's new head postman. Her employers reluctantly accepted her appointment "as an experiment", but long refused Mrs Baker the usual five shillings extra allowance.

Vera Brittain and Agatha Christie were among the 90,000 volunteers (the majority female) who joined the Red Cross Voluntary Aid Detachment (VADs) and served as nurses. Sixty Red Cross detachments were registered in Dorset before the war and there were Red Cross institutions and military hospitals across the county, making an invaluable contribution to the war effort. Many hospitals were established in the large houses of wealthy people. Mrs Percy Browne, for instance, fitted out her home as Fifehead Magdalen Voluntary Aid Hospital on her own initiative. She had eight beds for wounded servicemen and tended a total of 37 patients.

As well as wounded British servicemen, soldiers from allied nations and the Empire became a familiar sight in Dorset. Belgian soldiers were among the first. From 1915, Weymouth became a centre for wounded Australian and New Zealand servicemen, where they endeared themselves to the locals and stole a few hearts too.

Dorset women made many voluntary contributions to the war effort. This included welcoming and billeting Belgian refugees; visiting the sick and wounded in hospital; and organizing concerts. Many women sewed and knitted warm clothes for soldiers and sailors at home, others joined groups like the highly productive Easton Ladies' Sewing Circle. Women were also prominent in raising funds, including £1,600 for Dorset prisoners taken at Kut.

Women also found work in agriculture, though some conservative farmers doubted their ability to cope with long hours of hard labour and often preferred male German prisoners of war from the large POW camp outside Dorchester. This held 4,500 men and also supplied prison labour to several local trades and industries, as did two more POW camps near Blandford.

It was again a matter of gaining recognition. In a letter to the Editor of the Western Gazette of May 25th, 1917, Eleanor Grant, the County Organiser for the Dorset Board of Agriculture, describes how the Women's Land Army (formed that year) is "proving a great success…in coping with the great shortage of farm labour" and asks him to draw this to farmers' attention. Her message appears to have been heeded. By January 1918, 1,100 women were working on Dorset farms.

Feeding the Nation

Britain imported some 60% of its food in 1914: maintaining and increasing home food production was vital. Some people began stockpiling food at the outbreak of war, which inevitably led to shortages and price rises. Newspapers published notices like this from the Southern Times, August 1914: "The Weymouth Master Bakers' Association appeal to all their Customers to assist in this great National Crisis by TAKING ONLY THE USUAL QUANTITIES of BREAD and FLOUR…"

In the fields near Shaftesbury, sometime during World War I.

The British Government long resisted rationing, relying on appeals for voluntary restraint, whilst urging farmers and gardeners to produce more food. Not until July 1917 were householders issued with ration cards. These limited purchases of sugar to ½ lb per week. In 1918, rationing was extended to meat, butter, cheese and margarine.

The Royal Navy Cordite Factory at Holton Heath, Purbeck

Cordite is not a high explosive but a propellant used to fire artillery shells. It was made by combining another propellant, nitro-cellulose (guncotton), with the high explosive nitro-glycerine. In the early days of the process at Holton Heath it was done with the aid of the solvent acetone. It was laid in drying trays and rods or 'cords' were cut to length. Cordite was originally produced at Waltham Abbey but in 1914 Winston Churchill decided the Navy needed its own plant. Holton Heath was chosen as an ideal site; there were around 500 acres of heathland, close proximity to a main railway line and towns nearby to supply workers. The plant was up and working in nine months and over 2,000 people worked there at any one time. It was dangerous and dirty work and strict safety measures were in place. There was only one tragic accident; an explosion in a nitro-glycerine plant in 1931 killed ten people.

Women workers from the cordite factory at a social event.

The U-Boat War

Germany was well aware of Britain's vulnerable food security. The German surface fleet was heavily outnumbered by the Royal Navy, thus Germany relied much on submarines throughout the war to attack Allied warships and sink merchant vessels carrying vital food and war supplies. By the end of the war, German U-boats had sunk almost 5,000 ships.

Many of these lie off the Dorset coast, including HMS *Formidable*. Sailing from Portland, she was torpedoed 20 miles east of Start Point by U24 on New Year's Day, 1915. Of 780 sailors only 233 survived. It was Dorset's greatest naval tragedy of the war. Fifty men from *Formidable* were washed up in the ship's boat at Lyme Regis. One, John Cowen, was left for dead at the Pilot Boat Inn, but the landlord's collie, Lassie, licked his face and he revived.

The sea off Dorset became a new front line. Merchant ships carrying a variety of cargoes were sunk, even fishing boats were attacked. The waters around Portland Bill were a prime danger zone. One of many victims was *Valdes*, a Liverpool steamship of 2,223 tons carrying flour and hay for the Western Front, sunk on 18th February, 1917 seven miles off the Bill with the loss of 11 lives.

Germany resumed unrestricted U-boat warfare in 1917 and Admiral Sir John Jellicoe foresaw it might be impossible to continue the war in the face of rapidly mounting ship losses. Food stocks were dangerously low, Britain was close to being starved out; the Navy was short of fuel oil and many crews of neutral ships refused to call at vulnerable European ports.

In home waters, airships and seaplanes, including those from Naval Air Stations at Portland and Chickerell, and the airship bases at Upton,

HMS Formidable.

Left: The war memorial tablet in the church at Wimborne St Giles. It records the names of twenty-four men who died from this small village. Seven of these fought with the Dorsetshire Regiment in battalions that were heavily involved in fighting on the Western Front. Four of the men served with the Queen's Own Dorset Yeomanry and one with the newly formed Tank Corps.

Moreton and Toller Porcorum, were used to attack U-boats. The aircraft were also effective in forcing U-boats to submerge, where they could not fire their torpedoes and were virtually blind and immobile. After the development of depth charges in 1916, submerged submarines became vulnerable from Allied warships – often directed to their targets by the airmen.

However, it was the Royal Navy's belated adoption of the convoy system on May 24th, 1917, which proved decisive in reducing the terrible losses of Allied shipping and simultaneously increasing U-boat sinkings. This was militarily and politically essential, especially after the United States entered the war on April 6th. Of the 1.1 million American troops who sailed to Europe through 1917/18, only 637 were killed by submarine attacks.

Nonetheless, the threat of starvation remained. The Western Times of November 4th, 1917 reported a meeting of farmers at Dorchester Town Hall being told of "the dependence of the nation upon the farmer in the present crisis…" by the Secretary of the Board of Agriculture. He described how "…the enemy submarine had made it imperative to grow more food at home…." and urged farmers to turn as much as possible of their pasture to arable to drive up production and be "considerate" to the women (often from towns) who had taken the place of experienced farm workers.

Allied Naval Blockade

Meanwhile, the Allied naval blockade of Germany and Austria was starving the enemy of food and raw materials to wage the industrial war. An editorial in the Western Times of 2nd November 1918 headed "Sea Power" summarised the situation: "Those who would seem to have consistently lost sight of the fact that the Allied Fleet was the guarantee of final success have now a demonstration of what command of the sea really expresses. It matters not whether Germany continues to fight on land. Her fate will, in any event, be sealed by the sea power of the Allies."

The Armistice came nine days later. It was forced on Germany by blockade leading to deep and widespread political unrest verging on revolution and the abdication of the Kaiser, combined with the remarkable advances of the Allies on all fronts, especially the key Western Front, during the relentless Last Hundred Days campaign.

On land, at sea, in the new aerial war and on the home front, Dorset had played an honourable part in the victory, but at high cost in human life and suffering, as war memorials around the county testify. Langton Herring was Dorset's only "thankful village", grateful each of its 31 sons returned alive from the war. Other Dorset villages grieved for men who would never come back: 13 from Abbotsbury, for instance and 14 from Portesham: numbers that could be ill spared in small communities. Even these figures do not include deaths from influenza, which spread rapidly from troops to civilians through 1918 and became a world-wide pandemic, claiming more lives than all the battlefield casualties combined.

The unveiling of the Cann war memorial.

The Second World War

Preparing for War

Faced with German rearmament and Nazi aggression the British government rapidly - if belatedly - increased defence spending in the late 1930s, whilst pursuing the futile policy of Appeasement. In 1938, there were 381,000 in Britain's armed forces, which was doubled a year later. The Territorial Army was also doubled in size in 1939.

"Nearly 1¼ millions to be spent on armaments in Dorset" ran the Dorset County Chronicle's headline on 23rd March, 1939. This sum was for improved army accommodation at Bovington and Lulworth camps and the Dorsetshire Regiment's Dorchester Depot. A new tented camp was established on the WWI camp site at Blandford. Later, Bailey Bridges were designed there, which made an immense contribution to Allied advances in Italy and North-West Europe.

War appeared inevitable in 1939. Bombing of Britain's industrial cities was anticipated and by March the Dorchester Evacuation Committee was prepared for 4,612 evacuees. Dorset, with its strategic position on the Channel coast and defence capabilities, was a likely target too. It was one of 15 southern counties to test the Blackout, with practice fire drills in Bournemouth. Gas masks were issued and air raid shelters built.

On 9th August, 1939, King George VI reviewed the Reserve Fleet at Portland Naval Base, where defences had lately been strengthened. With 1,500 acres of enclosed harbour, Portland and its extensive facilities were of key strategic importance. Home of the Anti-Submarine Flotilla, it also undertook valuable work on Asdic, the anti-submarine detection apparatus.

The fleet at Portland 1939.

A Spitfire at Warmwell.

Other pre-war preparations that tense summer included RAF war games and tests of Britain's vital radar defence. Britain declared war on Germany on September 3rd and was faced with transforming itself rapidly to the demands of total war. Conscription, such a contentious issue in WWI, was reintroduced immediately.

It was obvious aircraft would play a big part in the war, but of Dorset's dozen wartime military airfields, only Chickerell, Portland and Warmwell existed at the start – and only Warmwell was fully operational. The Air Ministry requisitioned all private airfields at the outbreak of war. Airspeed's aircraft production factory made Christchurch airfield the most significant in Dorset. It went on to build Oxford training aircraft, de Havilland Mosquitoes and Horsa assault gliders, as well as converting Spitfires into Seafires.

Fortunately, civil aviation was strong in Britain: it contributed greatly to the war effort. Many technical developments were transferrable to military aircraft and civil aviation provided many trained pilots who later served with the wartime RAF, especially after the Civil Air Guard was formed in 1938. This offered would-be pilots a year's training for £10.

Aircraft factories were scattered around Britain. They built over 130,000 aircraft during the war, but fewer than 8,000 of these in 1939. Like other strategic industries, it was massively expanded. In its peak year, 1944, it produced 26,461 aircraft and employed 1.7 million people. The majority were women.

Evacuees

Having learnt from bitter experience of airship and aircraft raids in WWI, when 1,392 British civilian were killed and 3,390 injured, the Government anticipated the threat posed by the Luftwaffe and made detailed and ambitious evacuation plans. Operation Pied Piper was launched on 1st September, 1939. In its first three days, 1.5 million people were evacuated from Britain's major industrial cities and ports, including London, considered likely targets for German bombing raids. In England alone, the evacuees included over 600,000 unaccompanied children and 400,000 mothers of young children. Pregnant women, disabled people, teachers and carers swelled the numbers. It was a remarkable feat of organisation.

Dorset played host to a significant share - nearly 4,000 evacuees were sent to Dorchester alone. Smaller communities also received substantial numbers: Bridport had 800 evacuees and surrounding villages 600. For all involved, evacuation was profoundly memorable. Many children had never been parted from their parents before, never left home. This was a shock: so too was being billeted with strangers, often of a different social class, with a strange and unfamiliar lifestyle. The countryside, its animals and birds, were equally strange and bewildering, another country.

Some evacuees remember their experiences as an exciting adventure and thrived in their temporary foster homes with kind and welcoming hosts:

"Mostly, it was an idyllic time for me," one lady recalled in a BBC People's War interview in 2005. "I went to Sydling vicarage. The housekeeper cared for me as never before. Like many children from London, I was considered to be undernourished by the country folk and Miss Ridout set about fattening me up. My brother was totally spoilt at the farm…No wonder we both found it hard to settle back into London after the war."

Another London evacuee recalling her stay in rural Dorset (Charminster) said:

"I only once experienced any feeling of homesickness, although my parents deserve a lot of credit for that. They never gave any indication that my leaving home was anything but an exciting adventure, which I would be sure to enjoy. I was nearly eleven; we had never been apart before."

"They were a very down-to-earth family and kind to us," one former evacuee told researcher and author Gillian Mawson. "Aunt Ada used to walk around with an uncut loaf of bread under her arm and ask 'Are you hungry, duck?' and if we said 'Yes' she would cut us a slice and spread it with butter." However, many suffered homesickness and found the unfamiliar environment hard to cope with. Other former evacuees remember a cold reception and there were also cases of abuse.

"We attended school, but the local children were unfriendly. Our accents stood out and we were called 'incomers'…"

"It was hard to make friends in the village as they looked on Londoners as poor and strange. Whenever anything went wrong the Londoners always got blamed. It was a lonely time, but we got used to it after a while…"

Evacuation of endangered towns and cities was voluntary and some eligible for evacuation elected to stay at home. However, it was compulsory for homes in Reception Areas such as Dorset to accept assigned evacuees and designated hosts were compensated at the rate of 10/6d for the first child and 8/6d for subsequent children. The authorities assessed which homes were suitable on the accommodation available rather than the willingness (or otherwise) of hosts to receive evacuees.

Despite government calls, backed by a poster campaign, to 'leave the children where they are' many mothers and children returned to their urban homes when the anticipated Luftwaffe bombing campaign failed to materialise during the "Phoney War". By early 1940, it was estimated 80% of evacuees had left the relative safety of the countryside, but the German invasion of France and the launch of the Blitz brought a second wave of evacuations. Some 1.25 million people left endangered cities, including Plymouth, Glasgow, Birmingham, Manchester, Hull and Liverpool. Dorset received most evacuees from Southampton and London. The government's original planning for Operation Pied Piper was vindicated. A third wave of evacuations followed from June 1944, as Germany launched its V-weapons ("doodlebugs") against London and the south-east, bringing further death indiscriminately to heavily populated areas.

Women at War

As in WWI, British women found many jobs in wartime production and in posts vacated by men. In addition, many women contributed to the war effort with voluntary work, including a million who joined the Women's Voluntary Service (WVS), which operated canteens, reception and rest centres for servicemen and helped bombed and homeless families among many other tasks.

In early 1941, the Government obliged women aged 18 to 60 to register for war work. Female conscription began in December, 1941. Various exceptions were made, especially for mothers of young children and expectant mothers, but single "mobile" women aged between 20 and 30 were given the choice of joining the armed services, working in industry, or joining the Land Army.

Germany revived its WWI strategy of sustained U-boat attacks to blockade and starve Britain into submission. As before, it was essential to boost home food production, especially high yielding cereals and vegetables. The Dorset War Agricultural Committee proudly announced 31,000 acres of pasture had been ploughed in the county during 1940 and aimed for 22,000 acres more in 1941.

Once again, the Women's Land Army played a vital role. "Increasing Demand of Women Workers: More Volunteers Needed" announced the Western Gazette of April 12th, 1940:

The 'Timber Corps' of the Women's Land Army at work in the forests near Wareham.

"With the calling up of this year's age groups and the shortage of labour on the land, increased demands are being made on the Women's Land Army in Dorset. At the present moment there are 88 land girls working on Dorset farms and six others on training in approved farms. Mrs Heenan, the organising secretary for Dorset, told the Western Gazette that large numbers were still wanted for milking, horticultural and general farm work."

The Women's Land Army expanded rapidly. The Western Gazette reported two years later (13th November, 1942) on a rally at Sherborne: "...the guest of honour congratulated the Land Army on 'a first rate job…The Land Army now numbered more than 50,000 in employment, of whom Dorset claimed 699…it was not a county that took too kindly to the idea at first, but then Dorset was perhaps a little conservative.' (Laughter)."

The Dunkirk Evacuation and the Fall of France

We anticipate. The Phoney War came to a sudden and violent end on 10th May, 1940 when German forces invaded the Low Countries. Attacking through the Ardennes and the Somme Valley, the Germans achieved what they had failed to do in 1918 in splitting the bulk of British and French forces, driving the British into the sea and defeating France singly.

Meanwhile, the menace of the unfolding situation was brought home as dozens of overloaded Dutch vessels carrying refugees arrived in Poole. Across the Channel, the 2nd Dorsets were among British forces retreating rapidly before the German onslaught. After five terrible days and nights of marching and fighting, they withdrew under fire to the Mole at Dunkirk.

Pleasure boats from Bournemouth, Poole and Weymouth joined the hastily assembled armada of small ships which helped evacuate encircled

SS St Helier, Weymouth.

British, French and Belgian troops in Operation Dynamo. Portland contributed Motor Anti-Submarine boats MASB 6, 7 and 10 to the Dunkirk rescue, plus the trawlers *Kindred Star, Thrifty, Topaze, Olvina and Elina*. Among the casualties; Dorset vessel Island Queen was sunk and Skylark VI badly damaged.

Several crew of S.S. *St. Helier*, a steamship well known at Weymouth, were decorated for bravery. The Western Gazette of 14th June, 1940, celebrated the "heroic part played by the G.W.R. steamer SS *St Helier*….on the job for ten days, making eight journeys to Dunkirk and one to Calais. She experienced fierce bombing from Nazi planes and shelling from guns on the shore."

Poole's inshore lifeboat crew also distinguished themselves. The lifeboat's shallow draught allowed it to go right into the beaches, where it survived shore fire from Germans less than 40 yards away. Poole boats were again in action on 12th June, part of Operation Cycle, which rescued 3,321 soldiers from St Valery-en-Caux in Normandy.

Between 26th May and 4th June, 338, 226 Allied troops (215,000 of them British) were rescued from heavily bombarded and strafed beaches. Some 6,000 survivors, many French, were sent to Weymouth, as well as Belgian refugees and over 23,000 Channel Islanders fleeing the German invasion.

France fell; the Germans occupied airfields on the Cherbourg peninsula, only 70 miles from the Dorset coast, putting the county in the front line. On 3rd July, Bournemouth was bombed for the first time.

German aircraft attacked between Portland and Hengistbury Head, sinking four vessels and damaging nine more. Dive bombers then attacked Portland Harbour and sank two ships, including HMS *Foylebank*, killing 72 of her crew. Although mortally wounded, Jack Mantle continued firing his deck gun and won a posthumous Victoria Cross for his courage.

FOYLEBANK

HMS Foylebank.

Invasion Threatens

Invasion appeared imminent. As in WW1, the compelling demands of total war curtailed civil liberties and brought tighter social control. Rationing was re-introduced in July 1940 and made more extensive than in WW1, including petrol, clothing and furniture. Meanwhile, everyone living in Military Control Areas – which in Dorset included the entire coast and towns up to 20 miles inland – was issued with ID cards and movement was carefully restricted and controlled. Spy Mania reappeared. Even carrying a camera could lead to arrest. American journalist and broadcaster Ed Murrow was once arrested for asking too many questions about wartime life.

The Home Defence Executive's efforts concentrated on Britain's southern and eastern "coastal crust". Behind this, a network of 50 "stop lines" was constructed to shield the most heavily populated and industrialised areas and give defence in depth – a principle learned on the Western Front in WW1. In Dorset, the chief stop lines were the coast itself; the Taunton Stop Line connecting the English and Bristol Channels and the stop line running north from Bournemouth to Salisbury. A further stop line formed

Sherborne Home Guard, 1943.

a defensive ring stretching from Poole to Wimborne, Blandford, Sherborne and Yeovil, thence back to Poole via Dorchester and Wareham.

Stop lines utilised rivers and canals to impede the advance of infantry and (especially) motorised units, including tanks. These were supplemented with a variety of hastily improvised defences, including road and rail blocks, concrete pillboxes and anti-tank obstacles; gun and searchlight emplacements. A few of these defences survive today.

The Dorset coast was part of this prepared battlefield. Many miles of barbed wire entanglements were built and the beaches heavily mined: 3,500 mines were laid in just one mile of beach at Ringstead Bay. Similar quantities were buried at other beaches deemed prime targets for invasion, including Kimmeridge, Worbarrow, Swanage, Studland, Bournemouth and Barton-on-Sea.

HMS Turtle, an amphibious warfare centre with up to 4,000 personnel, was established at Poole, which was sealed off and its harbour defended with WW1 naval guns and a steel boom. A minefield was laid between Sandbanks and Brownsea Island. The Navy requisitioned six pleasure craft and armed them with machine guns. Meanwhile, Bovington Camp's unique collection of early WW1 tanks was used as pillboxes, or as scrap to feed the insatiable wartime hunger for metal. Huts were cleared from beaches at Poole, Bournemouth and Christchurch to give a clear field of fire; the central sections of Bournemouth and Boscombe piers were destroyed to prevent the enemy using them in an invasion. Road and railway signs and milestones were taken down to confuse invading Germans. Even the Cerne Giant was covered up as he might be a used as a navigational aid!

Most men not in the armed forces were involved in civil defence as ARP (Air Raid Precautions) wardens, rescue workers, special policemen, auxiliary firemen, ambulance drivers, firewatchers and in the Royal Observer Corps. The largest contingent - 1½ million - was the LDV (Local Defence Volunteers), later known as the Home Guard, created on 14th May, 1940. They initially relied on improvised weapons, including guns in private ownership, knives and bayonets on poles. Other rapidly produced devices included "sticky bombs" and grenades in bottles. However, the Home Guard gained uniforms in July; 500,000 modern Enfield rifles and 25,000 Browning automatic rifles; plus millions of rounds of ammunition bought from America. Winston Churchill proudly claimed Britain was a nation under arms.

A deterrent to invasion, the Home Guard also released regular troops for the front. Ultimately, there were seven Home Guard battalions in Dorset, operating vital coast artillery and anti-aircraft defences; manning road blocks; patrolling their area and checking identity cards. Meanwhile, small elite Home Guard units commanded by professional soldiers were secretly trained in guerrilla tactics. A memorial to one, the "Creech Barrow Seven", stands under Knowle Hill near Corfe Castle at SY933835.

Sherborne ARP wardens.

Britain's Home Defence System rested on RAF Fighter Command. Its RDF (Radio Direction Finding) stations were the first line of its integrated and very effective communications. Enemy aircraft crossing the coast were tracked by the Royal Observer Corps (ROC) – Dorset ultimately had 29 ROC posts. The vital information was collated, filtered, plotted on large scale maps and then relayed to fighter stations and on to their pilots.

Batteries were built all along the Dorset coast. Originally, there were four heavy anti-aircraft (AA) sites in Weymouth and four more at Holton Heath. By 1941 there were approximately 160 light AA sites along the Dorset coast, supported by 41 searchlight sites.

The Telecommunications Research Establishment (TRE) was operated in Worth Matravers from February 28th, 1940; before being transferred to Malvern, Worcestershire, in 1942 for extra security. Winston Churchill, who took over as Prime Minister from Neville Chamberlain on 10th May, 1940, realised TRE was essential for both the RAF's offensive and defensive operations, as well as Coastal Command's hunt for U-boats. TRE's complementary development of radio and radar jamming in the "Battle of the Beams" helped frustrate the Luftwaffe's efforts to pinpoint bombing targets and British aircraft.

The Battle of Britain

On 6th July, RAF Warmwell became a frontline airfield with the arrival of 609 Squadron and its Spitfires. They scrambled into action only three days

Telecommunications Research Establishment, Worth Matravers.

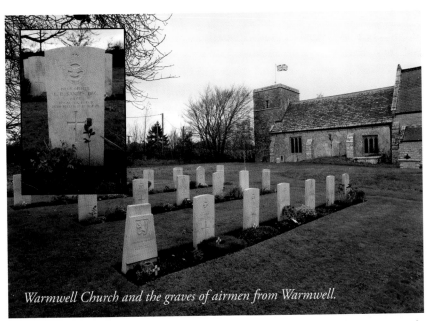

Warmwell Church and the graves of airmen from Warmwell.

later when dive bombers attacked Channel shipping off Portland. The Battle of Britain had begun. It lasted until the end of October and proved a major turning point in the war. The Luftwaffe's failure to win dominion of the skies over Britain so that Operation Sealion (the cross-Channel invasion of Britain) could be launched was its first big setback. It never fully recovered.

Although considerably outnumbered, the RAF's fighter pilots (14% of whom were from other parts of Europe and the Commonwealth) enjoyed a crucial advantage in flying over their homeland. Luftwaffe crews ran the gauntlet of anti-aircraft defences, barrage balloons and searchlights. German airmen faced capture if shot down or forced to bale out; British fliers returned to serve if they managed to bale out safely – almost 50% did; some more than once.

Most RAF fighter squadrons were equipped with Hurricanes and Spitfires, superb aircraft which had a considerable edge over the Messerschmitt Bf 110 fighter/bombers, though they met their match with Messerschmitt Bf 109s. Dogfights were a familiar sight in Dorset's skies. Many involved aircraft from RAF Warmwell. To take one page from Warmwell's wartime story: on 25th July, Spitfires of 152 Squadron brought down a Dornier Do.17 at East Fleet Farm. One of the accompanying Stukas was shot down by Flying Officer "Jumbo" Deansley, who was forced to bale out into the sea when his Spitfire was badly damaged. Fortunately, Deansley was picked up by SS *Empire Henchman* with only minor injuries.

"Der Kanalkampf", a concentrated attack on Allied shipping in and around the Channel and east coast ports, was the first phase of the Luftwaffe's campaign and lasted until 7th August. It exacted a heavy toll. Such was the loss of merchant shipping between Dorset and the Cherbourg peninsula, that the Admiralty suspended coastal convoys on 27th July. After HMS *Delight* was dive bombed and wrecked by Stukas off Portland Bill, the English Channel was placed off limits to destroyers in daytime.

German airmen then focussed their attacks on airfields, RDF stations, aircraft factories and south coast ports. Over 100 aircraft attacked Portland, dropping 32 bombs inside Admiralty property and three on the Navy's Torpedo Depot at Weymouth. By 1945, Portland would sustain 48 bombing raids, in which 532 bombs killed 34 civilians.

From the 24th August to 7th September 1940, the Luftwaffe concentrated on attacking fighter airfields. On 25th August, Enigma decrypts from the top secret code breaking centre at Bletchley Park warned RAF aerodromes at Warmwell, Little Rissington (Gloucestershire) and Abingdon to expect attack. Twelve Spitfires were scrambled from Warmwell, which was hit by 20 bombs only shortly afterwards. The Warmwell Spitfires were joined by Hurricanes from RAF Exeter in dogfights over Portland which cost both sides dearly.

After 7th September, the Luftwaffe switched their main focus to daylight raids on London and other cities. Spitfires from Warmwell defended the capital on September 15th at the height of the German campaign, a vain effort to sap Britain's resolve to fight on. Arguably (though such speculation has been widely disputed), this change of strategy enabled Fighter Command

An unexploded bomb, Dorchester.

Arming a Hurricane, Warmwell.

to hold out and win the Battle of Britain. Having failed to win air and naval superiority over Britain, his preconditions for invasion, Adolf Hitler postponed Operation Sealion indefinitely. Churchill knew this on 17th September through British Intelligence, but kept it secret for fear of alerting Germans to Bletchley Park's success at Enigma decryptions.

The Blitz

The Battle of Britain morphed into the Blitz, which was intense until May, 1941. RAF Warmwell continued to be one of the most active stations defending Britain. On October 21st, its 609 Squadron became the first Spitfire squadron to celebrate 100 victories – though Number 1 Squadron had achieved the same distinction with Hurricanes during the Battle of France.

As well as enormous destruction, the Blitz killed 43,000 British civilians and wounded another 139,000. Dorset was far from immune. The Luftwaffe targeted Westland's aircraft factory at Yeovil on September 30th, but blind bombing damaged 766 buildings in nearby Sherborne, destroying 10%. Eighteen civilians were killed. On 7th October, the Luftwaffe again targeted Westland, killing 100 workers in a direct hit on an air raid shelter. On their way they bombed Weymouth, hitting the bus depot and killing four civilians.

Worse was to come. On 14/15th November the Luftwaffe launched a massed raid of 449 aircraft on Coventry, killing over 500 citizens. Bournemouth was attacked the following night, killing 53 people and

Bomb damage, South Street, Sherborne.

A German Dornier shot down over Portland.

damaging 2,321 properties. The next day 12 died in a raid on Weymouth. Death continued to come suddenly from the skies. On 27th March, 1941, two bombs dropped by a lone German aircraft missed their railway target and struck Branksome Gas Works, killing 34 gathered in the canteen for lunch. On 1st April, three Heinkel He.111s attacked RAF Warmwell, killing 10 people and injuring 20.

Neither radar nor the Observer Corps had spotted the Heinkels. A radio direction beam from the Cherbourg peninsula guided the Luftwaffe through night skies to Coventry. Identifying where and when to expect attacks and foiling the enemy's aerial navigation was an ongoing battle.

Staff from TRE in Worth Matravers salvaged radio beam flying equipment from a Heinkel He.111 that crashed landed in West Bay. They worked out its operating frequency and distorted the signal. Sadly, this knowledge came too late to save Coventry, but it deflected a subsequent German raid from the vital Rolls Royce aero-engine plant in Derby.

TRE outgrew the facilities at Worth Matravers. An experimental model shop built near Bournemouth in 1941 developed the radar apparatus H2S, "the Magic Eye". The RPU (Research Prototype Unit) at West Howe, Bournemouth, continued its work and employed up to 700 people working seven day weeks.

Right: Radar memorial, St Aldhelm's Head.

War at Sea

Meanwhile, war raged at sea. HMS *Dorsetshire*, a heavy cruiser, was among the ships which sank the *Bismarck*, one of Germany's largest battleships, 300 miles west of Brest on 27th May, 1941. Transferred east, she was sunk with HMS *Cornwall* by Japanese dive bombers, 5th April, 1942. The HMS *Dorsetshire* Replacement Campaign launched by the Earl of Shaftesbury played a big part in Dorset's War Savings efforts and funded three minesweepers, HMS *Poole*, *Bridport* and *Lyme Regis*.

The Allies blockaded Germany from the outbreak of war, but German attacks on merchant shipping, Britain's lifeline (as in 1914-18), continued mercilessly throughout the war. Again, they were spearheaded by U-boats. Learning bitter lessons from WWI, the Allies used convoys in the Battle of the Atlantic, but suffered heavy losses nonetheless – a total of 3,500 merchant vessels (13.5 million tons), 175 naval ships and 741 aircraft.

Action off the Dorset coast included the Battle of Lyme Bay on 9th July, 1942, when the 1st Schnellboot Flotilla attacked Allied Convoy E/P 91. Seven German E-boats sank a total of 12,192 tons of merchant shipping, including tanker SS *Pomella*, four freighters and armed trawler HMT *Manor*. From 1943, the Allies gained the upper hand. More ships arrived safely in British ports whilst more U-boats were sunk, due in large part to improved radar. During the course of the war, Germany lost 783 U-boats, as well as 47 surface ships. Many submarines were destroyed by RAF Coastal Command, whose main bases were at Pembroke Dock and Mount Batten, Plymouth. From summer 1942, RAF Hamworthy flew many successful missions from Poole, using Short Sunderland and Catalina flying boats and focussing on the Bay of Biscay, a favoured U-boat hunting ground. They also flew air/sea rescue patrols and attacked surface ships.

Poole was already a base for BOAC flying boats, providing vital air links to the Americas, Africa, Australia and India, where the 2nd Battalion Dorset Regiment were posted in 1942. In April, 1944, the Dorsets were heavily engaged in the Battle of Kohima. This cost them 473 casualties, but began the XIV Army's advance that eventually cleared the Japanese from Burma.

Seaborne Attacks

On 19th August, 1942, a daring raid on Dieppe was launched from Weymouth to take and hold the heavily defended port and thus demonstrate the Allies' commitment to opening the Second Front and the liberation of Europe. Sadly, Allied covering fire was inadequate and the troops, mainly Canadian, were trapped on the beach by obstacles and German fire. Of 6,086 who took part, 3,623 were killed, wounded or taken prisoner. The Dieppe Raid proved how hard and costly any seaborne attack against strong defences would be, but gave valuable lessons for Operation Torch, the successful Anglo-American invasion of French North Africa in November 1942. Operation Husky, the Allied seaborne invasion of Sicily, came a year later. The island was taken in six weeks; Mussolini was toppled from power and large numbers of German troops diverted from the Eastern Front to defend Italy and the Balkans.

Aircraft from RAF Hurn plus Christchurch built gliders were involved in Husky and the 1st Battalion of the Dorsets were among the British contingent. The 1st Dorsets went on to fight in Italy and in the 1944 D Day landings on Gold Beach, Normandy.

Swanage Dairy, 1942.

Air Raids

Dorset continued to suffer air raids. German dive bombers killed 20 people and injured 56 as they swept across Weymouth on April 2nd, 1942. Two people were killed by bombs dropped on Bridport on 2nd August, 1942 and eight died and 39 were injured in a raid on Swanage, which was again bombed on 23rd August. Five died and nine were wounded. The town was attacked yet again on 3rd February, 1943 at the cost of four lives.

Five people were killed in Parkstone on 11th September, 1942 by a lone German plane. Further raids on Poole, Bridport and Lulworth Camp drove home the Luftwaffe's message of terror. Bournemouth endured its worst ever air raid on 23rd May, 1943: 101 people were killed. Several of the town's largest stores were destroyed and 24 airmen died as the Hotel Metropole collapsed. Another raid on Bournemouth killed 13 people and damaged over 1,400 properties on 12th August. Looking back from 8th December, 1944, the Bournemouth Times counted 2,271 bombs dropped on the town, killing 219 people and damaging or destroying 13,950 buildings.

Although the decoy on Brownsea helped save RAF Hurn and the cordite factory at Holton Heath and diverted an estimated 1,000 tons of bombs, Poole had been bombed 48 times by late 1944. According to the Western Times, (November 17th, 1944): "Since the first bomb was dropped in the Poole borough in June 1940, 240 incidents caused by incendiary and high explosive bombs have been reported. The death toll numbers 67, with a total casualty list of 38 seriously injured and 136 slightly hurt."

Taking the War to the Enemy

The potential for retaliatory air raids on Germany increased enormously after the United States entered the war on 7th December, 1941 and developed into a massive bombing campaign against Germany and targets in occupied Europe more terrible than the Blitz. More airfields were built, including Tarrant Rushton. Operational from May 1943, Tarrant was a base for Halifax heavy bombers, which were also used to tow Horsa and Hamilcar assault gliders.

British, American and Canadian pilots trained at Tarrant Rushton, which played several roles later in the war, including arms and supply drops to SOE (Special Operations Executive) and Resistance in France and the Resistance in Norway and Denmark. Paratroops flew from Tarrant on D-Day,

Warmwell airfield.

The perimeter track, Tarrant Rushton, today.

including the British 6th Airborne Division, the first to land in Normandy. They arrived by Horsa gliders towed by Halifaxes and took bridges over the Caen Canal, including Pegasus Bridge. Gliders and planes from Tarrant played a large part in landings on D-Day.

Dorset gained another airfield at Henstridge. This was commissioned as HMS Dipper in 1943 by the Fleet Air Arm. It trained pilots for the large RNAS base at nearby Yeovilton and gained an aircraft repair depot.

Meanwhile, the war behind the scenes continued in Dorset. TRE at Worth Matravers developed a simple but ingenious system called "Window", millions of aluminium foil strips dropped from the air which created a smokescreen effect on German radar. Forty tons of "Window" (92 million strips) were dropped to cloak a massed raid of 791 bombers on Hamburg and credited with saving 36 aircraft and their crews.

The "bouncing bomb" designed by Barnes Wallis was largely tested on Fleet Lagoon behind Chesil beach by aircraft flying from RAF Warmwell. Several test flights and design changes were made before the famous "Dambusters" raid on 16/17th May, 1943, which breached two dams in Germany's Ruhr valley, causing major flood damage and loss of life. The RAF lost eight aircraft and 53 aircrew.

RAF's Bomber Command suffered heavy casualties during the war: 55,573 aircrew were killed - a 44.4% death rate. Many aircraft were lost over the Channel, but the Western Gazette of 25th February, 1944 described how two gallant Abbotsbury fishermen in a small boat made three successful rescue sorties. Despite rough seas, they saved nine airmen whose plane had crashed a mile offshore.

Preparing for the Second Front, Operation Overlord

Dorset's largest contribution to winning the war was in the preparation for and execution of the Normandy landings in 1943/44 when the county became an armed camp. Dorset, along with Devon and Cornwall, hosted American troops, counties eastwards British and Canadian. More than 80,000 Americans were stationed in Dorset, in tented camps, barracks and billets.

The major part of the American assault forces on D-Day was launched form Weymouth and Portland, which were given over to US Force O for Omaha Beach. Between then and VE Day, 8th May, 1945, an astonishing 418,935 troops and 144,093 vehicles embarked from these harbours, plus vast amounts of war material. Many prisoners and Allied casualties were shipped back to Dorset ports.

It was a huge logistical achievement. Preparations began nine months before D-Day. Troops built twelve hutted camps and seven hospitals in Dorset; as well as supply depots; fuel and ammunition stockpiles; ordnance and repair shops; port facilities; airstrips; anti-aircraft gun positions; POW cages and a host of administrative facilities. They requisitioned 1,500 buildings around Dorset and took over and enlarged existing military bases, especially airfields. Portland was packed with landing craft: huge bulldozers carved out an enormous vehicle park and American engineers reinforced roads.

British landing craft taking US troops to ships off the Dorset coast.

US troops marching along the Esplanade, Weymouth, prior to D-Day.

Weymouth too was a large USNAAB base, with 2,500 men billeted in the Royal Hotel alone. In Poole, the Americans took over most of the quayside, requisitioning over 60 properties and stockpiling huge quantities of fuel, ammunition and supplies of all kinds. The US Navy assembled a fleet of landing craft in the harbour, setting up headquarters in the Dorset Yacht Club and 1,500 Americans moved into HMS Turtle.

Poole shipbuilders J Boslon and Son were Britain's leading builders of assault landing craft, constructing one every day in the build up to D-Day. The yards also produced Air-Sea rescue speedboats and minesweepers as well as repairing tank landing ships. Some sections of the artificial Mulberry Harbours, key to landing essential supplies, were secreted at Portland, where two caissons remain hard by Portland Castle.

Every Dorset town had its American Red Cross Club, but off-duty Americans often preferred local pubs and acquired a taste for warm beer and rough cider. British food - rationed and meagre - had little attraction, but civilians were impressed by abundant American supplies, which GIs were generous in sharing out.

Dorset had its fair share of the 70,000 British women who married GIs and the "friendly invasion" left many abiding memories. George Richards, then 11 years old recalled: "Many of us saw live Afro-Americans for the first time, in those days segregated into all-black units. These men were unfailingly polite and generous to us kids..."

D-Day Training

Of necessity, D-Day training was intensive. Not only was the task extremely hazardous, but many men (especially the Americans) had never seen battle. General Eisenhower, the Supreme Allied commander, insisted on training with live ammunition. Inevitably, men died in training, including 29 American engineers killed in the grounds of Sherborne Castle when an anti-tank mine exploded.

Elite units of the US Rangers and the British Commandos practised the cliff climbing skills they would need on D Day at Swanage and Burton Bradstock, whilst the main amphibious training area in Dorset was Studland Bay, where the heathland and beaches resembled the targeted Normandy beaches. Live fire manoeuvers culminated in a full scale landing exercise at Studland on 18th April, 1944, watched by the King, Eisenhower, Churchill and Mountbatten from Fort Henry observation post, which still overlooks the beach. The exercise showed up some problems and was repeated in May.

The Operation Tiger Disaster

Similar amphibious training took place at Slapton, a huge shingle beach in South Devon. A communications error led to "attacking" troops coming under live fire on 27th April. An unknown number of men were killed. A second practice landing at Slapton (Operation Tiger) was scheduled for the next day, but the convoy of eight large landing craft suffered a surprise attack from nine German E boats in Lyme Bay only ten miles off Portland Bill.

Although two ships had been assigned to protect the convoy, one was in Plymouth for repairs. HMS *Azalea* led the landing craft in a straight line, giving the fast German boats an easy target. Confusion ensued as *Azalea* was a British vessel, but the landing craft were American and operated on a different radio frequency to British Naval HQ. Two landing craft were sunk by enemy fire, one was set alight, but made it back to shore with heavy loss of life and a fourth was damaged. The German E boats escaped without loss of life.

Surprise was vital to D-Day success, thus all survivors were sworn

28 APRIL 1944
LYME BAY
749 DIED DURING D-DAY
TRAINING EXERCISE 'TIGER'
WHEN A CONVOY OF LSTs
WAS ATTACKED BY E-BOATS
OFF PORTLAND

24 DECEMBER 1944
ENGLISH CHANNEL
802 DIED WHEN THE TROOPSHIP
'LEOPOLDVILLE' WAS SUNK BY
A TORPEDO OFF CHERBOURG

to secrecy. There was great anxiety about missing officers who had top level secret knowledge of the D-Day invasion plans. It is possible the invasion would have been changed or postponed if their bodies had not been recovered.

Had the disaster become common knowledge at the time (it was reluctantly acknowledged long after the war) it would have been disastrous for the troops' confidence and their faith in the military leadership – who were no doubt anxious to preserve their reputations too. Upwards of 749 American servicemen died in the attack and 200 were wounded. By comparison, only 198 Americans were killed in the actual Utah Beach landings on 6th June.

The tragedy taught some hard lessons. Allied radio frequencies were standardised and new plans made to rescue survivors from the sea. Many had died of hypothermia, whilst others had drowned needlessly by placing their lifebelts around their waists, not under their arms and were pulled underwater headfirst by their heavy backpacks.

Tyneham Requisitioned

On 16th November 1943, Tyneham's 225 inhabitants were given three months to evacuate their homes so that the Purbeck village and the coast between Lulworth and Kimmeridge could be used by the military. It was mainly used to train American tank crews for the Omaha Beach landings.

Evacuation was hurried and painful, but the villagers were promised they could return. Although the Army gave up much of the land it had requisitioned in Purbeck after the war, it kept Tyneham as part of the firing ranges. Today, the deserted village is a time capsule, with photographs and memorabilia of early 20th century life.

Tyneham today.

US troops embarking landing craft in Weymouth harbour

D-Day, June 6th, 1944

Field Marshall Sir Alan Brooke confided his fears for Overlord (the invasion) in his diary "…it may well be the most ghastly disaster of the whole war. I wish to God it were safely over." Despite the massive Allied superiority in troop numbers, aircraft, ships and war material, as well as the remarkable success of Operation Fortitude (an elaborate programme of deception to convince German commanders the invasion would be aimed at the Pas de Calais with a second attack on Norway – thus diverting German troops and guns from the real targets), Brooke's anxiety was well founded. The Atlantic Wall included artillery, sand traps, pillboxes, anti-tank guns, hedgehogs and nutcracker mines. Assaulting open beaches with largely inexperienced men carried huge risks and the battle hardened Wehrmacht remained the most formidable fighting machine; heavily armed with excellent anti-tank and anti-personnel weapons and backed by Panzers.

As Churchill observed, D-Day was "much the largest thing we have ever attempted." The invasion began with 24,000 parachute and glider borne troops, including a contingent from Tarrant Rushton. Aerial and naval bombardment of the five invasion beaches followed to open the way for the landings themselves.

Weymouth Bay saw the greatest gathering of warships since the Reserve Fleet was dispersed in 1939. These joined the rest of the 6,488 vessels at the mid-Channel assembly point to form the largest armada in history. The Weymouth and Portland contingent then headed for Omaha, the

Above: US troops embarking at Weymouth.

strongest defensive position on the entire invasion sector. Hills and cliffs rose steeply behind the beach and the German bunkers were almost immune to direct frontal fire.

Many landing craft were lost in the rough seas at Omaha and the Americans were forced to make a Kitchener-like charge over the beach at the German fortifications. Eventually, the beachhead was secured, but at the cost of 2,000 casualties on the first day alone.

Further east, minesweeper HMS *Lyme Regis* helped clear a safe passage through to Sword Beach, whilst the Dorsetshire Regiment's 1st Battalion was first among British units that secured Gold Beach. The Dorsets achieved all their D-Day objectives, but suffered heavy casualties then and in the ensuing Normandy campaign, in which the 4th and 5th Battalions also fought.

Normandy's bocage country of small fields and high hedges was well suited to defence. The Allies won the Battle of Normandy at the cost of 37,000 dead and 173,000 wounded and owed much to complete air superiority, The Germans suffered heavily too: 240,000 casualties and 210,000 prisoners.

Towards Victory

The invasion did not end with D-Day: a formidable Allied task force sailed from Portland on 25th June and was instrumental in capturing Cherbourg. Dorset ports continued to play a vital role supplying troops fighting in Europe during 1944/45. Meanwhile, many wounded servicemen were shipped back to American military hospitals in Dorset (26,390 by September 15th alone), bringing home to everyone the price of invasion.

Dorset's 1st, 4th and 5th Battalions supported Operation Market Garden (17th to 25th September 1944), the Allies' attempt to force their way through the Netherlands into Germany and finish the war by Christmas. This involved large numbers of paratroops and centred on the Battle of Arnhem, made famous by the film 'A Bridge Too Far'. Forty Halifaxes, towing 13 Hamilcar and 27 Horsa gliders flew 92 sorties from Tarrant Rushton.

The Western Gazette of 17th November, 1944, celebrated the "magnificent heroism of a battalion of the Dorsetshire Regiment…prepared to sacrifice itself to save the remnants of the gallant Airborne garrison at Arnhem." Indeed, the 250 men of the 4th Dorsets enabled 2,400 troops to withdraw from the Arnhem bridgehead. Fewer than 100 Dorsets escaped and they had to swim for their lives under fire. Captain Lionel Queripel from Dorchester won a posthumous VC at Arnhem along with John Grayburn, a graduate of Sherborne School. Other Dorsets were involved in the successful attacks on the nearby bridges over the Meuse and Waal rivers, establishing a narrow corridor into the Netherlands.

The Dorsets went on to fight in Germany and the 1st Battalion were the first infantrymen to enter the Reich; whilst aircraft and gliders from Tarrant were involved in Operation Varsity, the successful crossing of the Rhine, March 24th, 1945. Victory in Europe was achieved on May 8th. Given the large part Dorset had played in the war, it was fitting that the VE celebrations included a special BBC broadcast from the New Inn, Piddletrenhide, by Ralph Wightman, who was born and raised in the village.

Above left: Weymouth war memorial and right:
The US World War II memorial in Weymouth.

Places to Visit

The Keep Museum, Dorchester.

Dorchester Keep Military Museum

Originally the gatehouse for the Dorsetshire Regiment's Depot Barracks, the Keep (1879) is now the museum of the Devon and Dorset Regiments and has much to offer anyone interested in military history. Barrack Road, Dorchester DT1 1RN, 01305 264066.

Nothe Fort, Weymouth

Nothe Fort preserves WWII artillery, including a 40mm Bofors gun and four 3.7 inch anti-aircraft guns. They attacked German bombers en route to Bristol, as well as defending Weymouth and Portland, especially important during D-Day operations. The fort also served as a wartime ammunition store. The fort has many interesting displays, most relating to coastal defence and local military history, plus a programme of historical re-enactments and gun firings. Nothe Fort, Barrack Road, Weymouth DT4 8UF, 01305 766626.

Studland Bay

A 2km (1.3 mile) walk around Studland includes Dragon's Teeth anti-tank defences at Middle Beach (SZ036830); Fort Henry observation bunker (SZ 037828); the Bankes Arms (a control base) and the concrete pillbox on South Beach (SZ038828). Download a route description www.nationaltrust.org.uk/studlandbeach/trails/studland-beach-second-world-war-walk.

The Tank Museum

Dorset played a large part in the development of tanks (page 8) and training

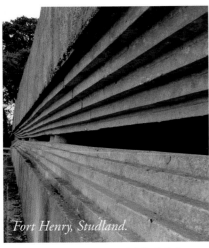

Fort Henry, Studland.

WWII defences, Studland.

tank crews. Bovington's Tank Museum traces the history of tanks with almost 300 vehicles from many countries. Linsay Rd, Bovington, Wareham BH20 6JG, 01929 405096.

Tyneham (see page 40)
Public access to the ranges is limited to weekends, public and school holidays. Always check on 01929 404819 before visiting.

Further Souvenirs of Wartime Dorset
Dorset's many bomb sites have been cleared, but the military camps at Bovington, Blandford and Lulworth survive. There are memorials too, including the lych gate at Hamworthy parish church to the Royal Marine

3.7inch heavy anti-aircraft gun, Nothe Fort.

Support Squadron; the Portland Memorial Tablet in Victoria Gardens; the column on Weymouth Esplanade and the RAF Warmwell memorial.

Among Dorset's wartime airfields, Hurn is now an international airport, whilst Henstridge is a small private airfield. The Henstridge control tower survives as a residential house, as does the Warmwell control tower. Warmwell's NAAFI/cinema/gym is now the village hall, but Warmwell's airfield has been built over, as has Christchurch's. Tarrant Rushton is now used for farming.

Dragon's teeth at Studland.

The remains of coastal defences can still be seen along many sections of the Dorset coast. Sheltered bays and gently sloping beaches had to be protected by 'dragon's teeth' when the threat of invasion was very real. Gun emplacements or 'pill boxes' are also still visible. Dorset is lucky to be the home of a number of excellent museums. Several of the larger ones were mentioned on the previous pages but others will provide a rewarding experience for those interested in Dorset's wartime heritage. The Swanage Museum and Heritage Centre has much information about the development of radar at the Telecommunications Research Establishment at Worth Matravers. Wareham Museum has a fascinating display about the town in World War I. Gold Hill Museum in Shaftesbury has a website devoted to memories of the town in the Great War and Sherborne Museum has exhibits and a wonderful collection of archive photographs from the two world wars. Portland Museum too has an extensive photograph collection.

Tyneham village is a moving reminder of wartime sacrifices.

Above: Tarrant Rushton airfield is now farmland but two hangars still remain as well as the perimeter road which is a public footpath. A small memorial at the entrance (inset) commemorates all who served there. The first troops to land in France on D-Day left from here on the night of June 5th, 1944.

48

Acknowledgements and photograph credits

Many thanks to Sherborne Museum, Gold Hill Museum, Shaftesbury, Swanage Museum and Heritage Centre, Portland Museum, Wareham Museum, The Keep Museum, Dorchester, Dave Fagan from the 'Hampshire Airfields' website and Cherish Watton from womenslandarmy.co.uk for their help and support in obtaining images and information.

Photographs
Wareham Museum, cover bottom and top left, p. 6, 7, 11, 14 and this page.
Sherborne Museum, cover top right, p. 9, 10, 26, 27 and 31.
The Keep Museum, Dorchester, p. 5 and 30 bottom left.
Gold Hill Museum, Shaftesbury, p. 4, 13 and 17.
Lyme Regis Museum, p. 15.
Hampshire Airfields, p. 19, 30 bottom right and 35.
Portland Museum, p. 18, 25, and 32 top.
womenslandarmy.co.uk, p. 22 (Joan and Geoff Shutte archive) and p. 23.
Swanage Museum and Heritage Centre, p. 28 and 34.
US National Archive, p. 37, 38 (12008267), 41 and 42 (12008272).
Robert Hesketh, p. 32 bottom, 40, 44, 45, 46 top and back cover.
Robert Westwood, p.29, 36, 39, 43, 46 bottom and 47.

Select Bibliography
British Newspaper Archive www.britishnewspaperarchive.co.uk
Dorset History Centre, Bridport Rd, Dorchester DT1 1RP.
Hesketh, Robert, Dorset's Castles and Fortifications, Inspiring Places Publishing, Alderholt, 2017.
Forty, George, Frontline Dorset, Dorset Books, Tiverton, 1994.
Legg, Rodney, Dorset in the First World War, Halsgrove, Wellington, 2012.
Legg, Rodney, Dorset at War, Halsgrove, Wellington, 2009.
Smith, Graham, Dorset Airfields in the Second World War, Countryside Books, Newbury, 1999.
Wadsworth, Jacqueline, Weymouth, Portland and Dorchester in the Great War, Pen and Sword, Barnsley, 2015
Westwood, Robert, The Tyneham Story, Inspiring Places Publishing, 2014 and 2017.